The Christmas
CAMEL

MICKEY MAGEE

Published By:
Jasher Press & Co.
www.jasherpress.com
customerservice@jasherpress.com
1.888.220.2068
New Bern, NC 28562

Copyright© 2014
Interior Text Design by Pamela S. Almore
Cover Design by Pamela S. Almore

ISBN: 978-0692457139

First Edition
Printed and bound in the United States of America

The Christmas
CAMEL

MICKEY MAGEE

JASHER PRESS AND CO.

DEDICATION

F or many years I have set up our family's
Christmas Nativity scene. Those figurines were
gifts from my Grandmother and the set up was
always completed when I placed the Christmas
Camel looking over Baby Jesus in the manger.

This book is dedicated to the Christmas Camel
because no one ever wrote a story about the
Christmas Camel.

You've heard of the "Little Drummer Boy",
"The Littlest Angel" too.
Those stories of Christmastime
Thrill us through and through.

Let's not forget the cow's warm breath,
Upon that infant child,
Nor the donkey's gentle bray
As the child lay sleeping…
in the hay.

The Shepherds came with footsteps soft,
some holding their pure white charges aloft...
upon shoulders broad and strong.
These gentle, weathered men
came on bended knee
To worship "The Great Shepherd"
Who one day would die for you and me.

His birth in a stable in Bethlehem town,
was heralded by angels
and heard for miles around.
While others saw a star
in the heavens so dark
and realized at once
upon a trip to the West they must embark.

These three kings from Orient far
mounted their camels
to follow that star.

It burned bright before them
as they sailed those desert seas
upon the backs of gentle camels
whose main job was to please.

And carry they did
Through wind, sand and rain
those three rich and wealthy Wise Men
who from the east came.
Never a whimper, a grumble nor snort
did one of those camels utter…
I can report.

Their rolling gait went on and on.
They seldom saw water
or a patch of unsandy land.

Their rolling gait went on and on.
They seldom saw water
or a patch of unsandy land.

In all the books you've ever read
about the Three Wise Men
there's a picture of a camel
sometimes two or three.
But the one we all remember
as before the crib it stands
is the camel standing quietly beside a Wiseman
who holds its bridle in his hand.

This camel has no name
but was there just the same
offering its praise and welcome
to that infant of Bethlehem.

He'd travelled far
with burdens quite heavy
but never uttered a word to his rider
that was in any way contrary.
He just did his job
Humbling plodding along.
It made no difference where,
someone please help him to stay strong.

But when he arrived at that stable
small, dark and dreary
a light shone from within
and angels sang songs;
happy, gay and cheery.

"Joy to the World" was their happy refrain,
The humble, quiet camel asked
"Why does such joy abound in this stable dark and
dreary?"
"A child is born. Emmanuel's his name!
God is with us.
We no longer need feel shame."

"How can that be?"
Said the camel with glee,
"since he did it for you will he do it for me?"

"Of course he will.
Rest assured
His grace is sufficient
For all to enjoy."

"Just accept the gift of freedom
From sin's wrath.
His death on a cross will be your life raft.
So give him your life
and the Lord of it he'll be.
Your paths he'll make smooth
Whether by day or by night
and you'll praise Him each day
For His burden is light."

"But I'm just a camel
hardly worth very much.
Why would he do that for me?
I'm just one of the bunch."

"Because you are a special,
one of a kind.
Before you were born
your life was on His mind.
So trust in his love
and follow his path.
It's planned to the very last inch
and with him it's a cinch.

"Thanks for the Good News"
Said the camel that night,
"Merry Christmas to all and to all a good night."

The Christmas Camel written
By Mickey Magee on
December 7, 2008
Because no one ever wrote about the Christmas
Camels of the Wise Men before…

Is there a book inside of you? Ever wanted to self publish but didn't know how? Concerned about the financial part of self publishing? Relax. Take a deep breath. We can help!

Finally! An affordable Self Publishing company for all of your Self Publishing needs. We have the right services, with the right prices with the right quality. So, what are you waiting for?

Unpack those dreams, break out that pen, your dreams of getting published may not be so far off after all!

Jasher Press & Co. is here to provide you with Consulting, Book Formatting, Cover Designs, editing services but most importantly inspiration to bring your dreams to past.

And this whole process can be done in less than 90 days! You thought about it, you talked about it but now is the time!

Made in the USA
Charleston, SC
27 May 2015